Put a little softness underfoot any place in your home with plush half-circle rugs. Ten crochet designs by Karen Barnes whip up in no time with chunky yarns and a big hook. Go for a classic allover pattern or add whimsy with antlers, flip-flops, or other appliqués.

LEISURE ARTS, INC.
Maumelle, Arkansas

# Puff Stitch

EASY

**Finished Size:** 33½" wide x 18½" deep (85 cm x 47 cm)

## SHOPPING LIST

### Yarn (Super Bulky Weight)

**[**4 ounces, 64 yards
(113 grams, 59 meters) per
skein**]**:

☐ 6 skeins

### Crochet Hook

☐ Size Q (16 mm)
**or** size needed for gauge

### Additional Supplies

☐ Puffy fabric paint (optional)

## GAUGE INFORMATION

**Gauge Swatch:**
7¾" wide x 4¼" high
(19.75 cm x 10.75 cm)
Work same as Rug for 3 rows:
17 sc.

## STITCH GUIDE

**PUFF ST** (uses one st)
★ YO, insert hook in st indicated, YO and pull up a loop even with loop on hook; repeat from ★ once **more**, YO and draw through all 5 loops on hook.

## RUG

**Row 1** (Wrong side)**:** Holding two strands of yarn together, ch 4, 6 dc in fourth ch from hook **(3 skipped chs count as first dc)**: 7 dc.

**Row 2:** Ch 1, turn; hdc in first dc, ch 2, (work Puff St in next dc, ch 2) across to last dc, hdc in last dc: 7 sts and 6 ch-2 sps.

**Row 3:** Ch 1, turn; sc in first hdc, (2 sc in next ch-2 sp, 3 sc in next ch-2 sp) across to last hdc, sc in last hdc: 17 sc.

**Row 4:** Ch 1, turn; hdc in first sc, ch 2, ★ skip next sc, work Puff St in next sc, ch 2; repeat from ★ across to last 2 sc, skip next sc, hdc in last sc: 9 sts and 8 ch-2 sps.

**Row 5:** Ch 1, turn; sc in first hdc, (2 sc in next ch-2 sp, 3 sc in next ch-2 sp) across to last hdc, sc in last hdc: 22 sc.

**Row 6:** Ch 1, turn; hdc in first sc, ★ ch 2, skip next sc, work Puff St in next sc; repeat from ★ across to last sc, hdc in last sc: 12 sts and 10 ch-2 sps.

**Row 7:** Ch 1, turn; sc in first hdc, 3 sc in each ch-2 sp across to last hdc, sc in last hdc: 32 sc.

**Row 8:** Ch 1, turn; hdc in first sc, ★ ch 2, skip next sc, work Puff St in next sc; repeat from ★ across to last sc, hdc in last sc: 17 sts and 15 ch-2 sps.

**Row 9:** Ch 1, turn; sc in first hdc, 2 sc in next ch-2 sp, (3 sc in next ch-2 sp, 2 sc in next ch-2 sp) across to last hdc, sc in last hdc: 39 sc.

**Row 10:** Ch 1, turn; hdc in first sc, ch 2, ★ skip next sc, work Puff St in next sc, ch 2; repeat from ★ across to last 2 sc, skip next sc, hdc in last sc: 20 sts and 19 ch-2 sps.

**Row 11:** Ch 1, turn; sc in first hdc, 2 sc in next ch-2 sp, (3 sc in next ch-2 sp, 2 sc in next ch-2 sp) across to last hdc, sc in last hdc: 49 sc.

**Row 12:** Ch 1, turn; hdc in first sc, ch 2, ★ skip next sc, work Puff St in next sc, ch 2; repeat from ★ across to last 2 sc, skip next sc, hdc in last sc: 25 sts and 24 ch-2 sps.

**Row 13:** Ch 1, turn; sc in first hdc, (2 sc in next ch-2 sp, 3 sc in next ch-2 sp) across to last hdc, sc in last hdc: 62 sc.

**Row 14:** Ch 1, turn; hdc in first sc, ★ ch 2, skip next sc, work Puff St in next sc; repeat from ★ across to last sc, hdc in last sc: 32 sts and 30 ch-2 sps.

**Row 15:** Ch 1, turn; sc in first hdc, (2 sc in next ch-2 sp, 3 sc in next ch-2 sp) across to last hdc, sc in last hdc: 77 sc.

**Row 16:** Ch 1, turn; hdc in first sc, ch 2, ★ skip next sc, work Puff St in next sc, ch 2; repeat from ★ across to last 2 sc, skip next sc, hdc in last sc: 39 sts and 38 ch-2 sps.

**Row 17:** Ch 1, turn; sc in first hdc, 2 sc in each ch-2 sp across to last hdc, sc in last hdc: 78 sc.

**Edging Rnd:** Ch 1, turn; sc in first sc, ch 3, dc in next sc, ★ skip next 2 sc, sc in next sc, ch 3, dc in next sc; repeat from ★ across to last 3 sc, skip next 2 sc, sc in last sc, ch 3; working in end of rows, dc in next sc row, sc in next hdc row, ch 3, [dc in next sc row, skip next hdc row, sc in next sc row, ch 3, dc in next hdc row, skip next sc row, sc in next hdc row, ch 3] twice, dc in next sc row, skip next hdc row, sc in next dc row, ch 3, dc in free loop of beginning ch *(Fig. 1, page 45)*, sc in next dc row, ch 3, dc in next hdc row, skip next sc row, sc in next hdc row, ch 3, dc in next sc row, [skip next hdc row, sc in next sc row, ch 3, dc in next hdc row, skip next sc row, sc in next hdc row, ch 3, dc in next sc row] twice; join with slip st to first sc, finish off.

**Optional:** Paint large dots on wrong side of rug for a non-slip surface.

# Lazy Puff Stitch

EASY

**Finished Size:** 39½" wide x 23" deep (100.5 cm x 58.5 cm)

## SHOPPING LIST

### Yarn (Super Bulky Weight)

SUPER BULKY 6

[4 ounces, 64 yards
(113 grams, 59 meters) per
skein]:

☐ 8 skeins

### Crochet Hook

☐ Size Q (16 mm)
**or** size needed for gauge

### Additional Supplies

☐ Puffy fabric paint (optional)

## GAUGE INFORMATION

**Gauge Swatch:** 8" wide x 4" high
(20.25 cm x 10 cm)

Work same as Rug, page 8, for 2 rows: 5 Puff Sts, 3 dc, and one ch-1 sp.

## STITCH GUIDE

**PUFF ST** (uses one st or sp)
Dc in st or sp indicated, ch 3, ★ YO, insert hook around post of dc just made ***(Fig. A)***, YO and pull up a loop, YO and draw through 2 loops on hook; repeat from ★ 2 times **more**, YO and draw through all 4 loops on hook.

**Fig. A**

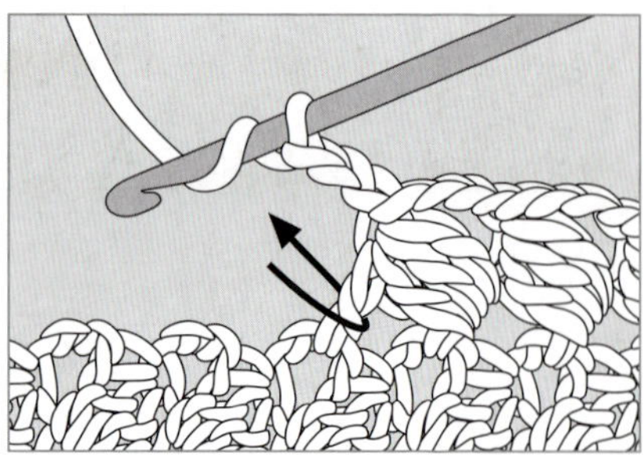

## RUG

**Row 1** (Wrong side)**:** Holding two strands of yarn together, ch 4, 6 dc in fourth ch from hook **(3 skipped chs count as first dc)**: 7 dc.

**Row 2:** Ch 4 **(counts as first dc plus ch 1, now and throughout)**, turn; work Puff Sts in each of next 5 dc, 2 dc in last dc: 5 Puff Sts, 3 dc, and one ch-1 sp.

**Row 3:** Ch 4, turn; work Puff St in next dc, work Puff St in ch-3 sp of each Puff St across to next ch-1 sp, dc in next ch-1 sp and in last dc: 6 Puff Sts, 3 dc, and one ch-1 sp.

**Row 4:** Ch 4, turn; work Puff St in next dc, ★ work 2 Puff Sts in ch-3 sp of next Puff St, work Puff St in ch-3 sp of next Puff St; repeat from ★ 2 times **more**, dc in next ch-1 sp and in last dc: 10 Puff Sts, 3 dc, and one ch-1 sp.

**Row 5:** Ch 4, turn; work Puff St in next dc and in ch-3 sp of next Puff St, ★ work 2 Puff Sts in ch-3 sp of next Puff St, work Puff St in ch-3 sps of next 2 Puff Sts; repeat from ★ 2 times **more**, dc in next ch-1 sp and in last dc: 14 Puff Sts, 3 dc, and one ch-1 sp.

**Row 6:** Ch 4, turn; work Puff St in next dc and in ch-3 sp of each Puff St across to next ch-1 sp, dc in next ch-1 sp and in last dc: 15 Puff Sts, 3 dc, and one ch-1 sp.

**Row 7:** Ch 4, turn; work Puff St in next dc and in ch-3 sps of next 2 Puff Sts, work 2 Puff Sts in ch-3 sp of next Puff St, ★ work Puff St in ch-3 sps of next 3 Puff Sts, work 2 Puff Sts in ch-3 sp of next Puff St; repeat from ★ once **more**, work Puff St in ch-3 sps of next 4 Puff Sts, dc in next ch-1 sp and in last dc: 19 Puff Sts, 3 dc, and one ch-1 sp.

**Row 8:** Ch 4, turn; work Puff St in next dc and in ch-3 sps of next 3 Puff Sts, work 2 Puff Sts in ch-3 sp of next Puff St, ★ work Puff St in ch-3 sps of next 4 Puff Sts, work 2 Puff Sts in ch-3 sp of next Puff St; repeat from ★ once **more**, work Puff St in ch-3 sps of next 5 Puff Sts, dc in next ch-1 sp and in last dc: 23 Puff Sts, 3 dc, and one ch-1 sp.

**Row 9:** Ch 4, turn; work Puff St in next dc and in ch-3 sps of next 4 Puff Sts, work 2 Puff Sts in ch-3 sp of next Puff St, ★ work Puff St in ch-3 sps of next 5 Puff Sts, work 2 Puff Sts in ch-3 sp of next Puff St; repeat from ★ once **more**, work Puff St in ch-3 sps of next 6 Puff Sts, dc in next ch-1 sp and in last dc: 27 Puff Sts, 3 dc, and one ch-1 sp.

**Edging Rnd:** Ch 4, turn; work Puff St in next dc and in ch-3 sps of next 5 Puff Sts, work 2 Puff Sts in ch-3 sp of next Puff St, ★ work Puff St in ch-3 sps of next 6 Puff Sts, work 2 Puff Sts in ch-3 sp of next Puff St; repeat from ★ once **more**, work Puff St in ch-3 sps of next 7 Puff Sts, dc in next ch-1 sp and in last dc; work Puff St in end of each row across; join with slip st to dc of first Puff St, finish off.

**Optional:** Paint large dots on wrong side of rug for a non-slip surface.

# Circle Rug

EASY

**Finished Size:** 43½" wide x 20½" deep (110.5cm x 52 cm)

## SHOPPING LIST

### Yarn (Jumbo Weight)

[5.29 ounces, 46 yards (150 grams, 42 meters) per skein]:

- ☐ Tan - 3 skeins
- ☐ Pink - 3 skeins

### Crochet Hook

- ☐ Size Q (16 mm) **or** size needed for gauge

### Additional Supplies

- ☐ Puffy fabric paint (optional)

## GAUGE INFORMATION

**Gauge Swatch:**
7" wide x 3½" high (17.75 cm x 9 cm)
Work same as Rug, page 12, for 2 rows: 12 dc.

## STITCH GUIDE

**DOUBLE CROCHET 4 TOGETHER** *(abbreviated dc4tog)* (uses next 4 sts)
★ YO, insert hook in **next** st, YO and pull up a loop, YO and draw through 2 loops on hook; repeat from ★ 3 times **more**, YO and draw through all 5 loops on hook **(counts as one dc)**.

**DOUBLE CROCHET 7 TOGETHER** *(abbreviated dc7tog)* (uses next 7 sts)
★ YO, insert hook in **next** st, YO and pull up a loop, YO and draw through 2 loops on hook; repeat from ★ 6 times **more**, YO and draw through all 8 loops on hook **(counts as one dc)**.

## RUG

**Row 1** (Right side)**:** With Tan, ch 4, 6 dc in fourth ch from hook **(3 skipped chs count as first dc)**: 7 dc.

***Note:*** Loop a short piece of yarn around any stitch to mark Row 1 as **right** side.

**Row 2:** Ch 3 **(counts as first dc, now and throughout)**, turn; 2 dc in each of next 5 dc, dc in last dc: 12 dc.

**Row 3:** Ch 1, turn; sc in first 2 dc, skip next dc, 7 dc in next dc, skip next dc, sc in next 3 dc, skip next dc, 7 dc in next dc, skip next dc, 2 sc in last dc: 21 sts.

**Row 4:** Ch 3, turn; beginning in first sc, dc4tog, ch 3, sc in next 3 dc, ch 3, dc7tog, ch 3, sc in next 3 dc, ch 3, dc4tog, dc in last dc (same st as decrease): 11 sts and 4 ch-3 sps.

**Row 5:** Ch 3, turn; 3 dc in next dc, skip next ch-3 sp, sc in next 3 sc, skip next ch-3 sp, 7 dc in next dc, skip next ch-3 sp, sc in next 3 sc, skip next ch-3 sp, 3 dc in next dc, dc in last dc: 21 sts.

**Row 6:** Ch 1, turn; sc in first dc, (2 sc in next st, sc in next st) across: 31 sc.

**Row 7:** Ch 1, turn; sc in first 2 sc, skip next sc, 7 dc in next sc, ★ skip next sc, sc in next 3 sc, skip next sc, 7 dc in next sc; repeat from ★ across to last 3 sts, skip next sc, sc in last 2 sc; finish off: 51 sts.

**Row 8:** With **wrong** side facing, join Pink with dc in first sc ***(see Joining With Dc, page 44)***; beginning in same sc, dc4tog, ch 3, sc in next 3 sts, ★ ch 3, dc7tog, ch 3, sc in next 3 sts; repeat from ★ across to last 4 sts, ch 3, dc4tog, dc in last sc (same st as decrease): 23 sts and 10 ch-3 sps.

**Row 9:** Ch 3, turn; 3 dc in next dc, skip next ch-3 sp, sc in next 3 sc, skip next ch-3 sp, ★ 7 dc in next dc, skip next ch-3 sp, sc in next 3 sc, skip next ch-3 sp; repeat from ★ across to last 2 dc, 4 dc in next dc, dc in last dc; finish off: 52 sts.

**Row 10:** With **wrong** side facing, join Tan with sc in first dc ***(see Joining With Sc, page 44)***; sc in next 2 dc, 2 sc in next dc, (sc in next 3 sts, 2 sc in next st) across to last 4 dc, sc in last 4 dc: 64 sc.

**Row 11:** Ch 1, turn; sc in first 2 sc, skip next 2 sc, 7 dc in next sc, ★ skip next 2 sc, sc in next 3 sc, skip next 2 sc, 7 dc in next sc; repeat from ★ across to last 3 sc, skip next sc, sc in last 2 sc; finish off: 81 sts.

**Rows 12 and 13:** Repeat Rows 8 and 9: 82 sts.

**Row 14:** With **wrong** side facing, join Tan with sc in first dc; sc in next 3 dc, 2 sc in next dc, (sc in next 4 sts, 2 sc in next st) across to last 7 sts, sc in last 7 sts: 97 sc.

**Row 15:** Ch 1, turn; sc in first 2 sc, skip next 2 sc, 7 dc in next sc, ★ skip next 3 sc, sc in next 3 sc, skip next 3 sc, 7 dc in next sc; repeat from ★ across to last 2 sc, sc in last 2 sc; finish off: 101 sts.

**Rows 16 and 17:** Repeat Rows 8 and 9: 102 sts.

**Trim:** With **right** side facing and working in end of rows, join Tan with sc in first row; ch 3, dc in same row, ★ skip next row, (sc, ch 3, dc) in next row; repeat from ★ across to last row, slip st in top of dc on last row; finish off.

**Optional:** Paint large dots on wrong side of rug for a non-slip surface.

# Semi-Circle

EASY

**Finished Size:** 41½" wide x 20" deep (105.5 cm x 51 cm)

## SHOPPING LIST

### Yarn (Jumbo Weight) JUMBO 7

**[**5.29 ounces, 46 yards (150 grams, 42 meters) per skein**]**:

- ☐ 5 skeins

### Crochet Hook

- ☐ Size Q (16 mm) **or** size needed for gauge

### Additional Supplies

- ☐ Puffy fabric paint (optional)

## GAUGE INFORMATION

**Gauge Swatch:**
10" wide x 4" deep
(25.5 cm x 10 cm)
Work same as Rug for 3 rows:
19 sts.

## RUG

**Row 1** (Right side)**:** Ch 4, 6 dc in fourth ch from hook **(3 skipped chs count as first dc)**: 7 dc.

**Row 2:** Ch 3 **(counts as first dc, now and throughout)**, turn; dc in next dc, ch 3, dc in next 3 dc, ch 3, dc in last 2 dc: 7 dc and 2 ch-3 sps.

**Row 3:** Ch 3, turn; 2 dc in first dc, sc in next dc, 5 dc in next ch-3 sp, skip next dc, sc in next dc, skip next dc, 5 dc in next ch-3 sp, sc in next dc, 3 dc in last dc: 19 sts.

**Row 4:** Ch 3, turn; dc in next dc, ch 3, skip next dc, 3 dc in next sc, ch 3, skip next dc, dc in next 3 dc, ch 3, skip next 3 sts, dc in next 3 dc, ch 3, skip next dc, 3 dc in next sc, ch 3, skip next dc, dc in last 2 dc: 16 dc and 5 ch-3 sps.

**Row 5:** Ch 1, turn; sc in first 2 dc, 5 dc in next ch-3 sp, ★ skip next dc, sc in next dc, 5 dc in next ch-3 sp; repeat from ★ across to last 2 dc, sc in last 2 dc: 33 sts.

**Row 6:** Ch 3, turn; dc in first sc, ch 3, skip next 2 sts, dc in next 3 dc, ch 3, ★ skip next 3 sts, dc in next 3 dc, ch 3; repeat from ★ across to last 3 sts, skip next 2 sts, 2 dc in last sc: 19 dc and 6 ch-3 sps.

**Row 7:** Repeat Row 5: 39 sts.

**Row 8:** Ch 3, turn; dc in first sc, ch 3, ★ skip next 2 sts, dc in next 3 sts, ch 3; repeat from ★ across to last 3 sts, skip next 2 sts, 2 dc in last sc: 25 dc and 8 ch-3 sps.

**Row 9:** Repeat Row 5: 51 sts.

**Row 10:** Ch 3, turn; dc in first sc, ★ ch 3, skip next 2 sts, dc in next 3 sts; repeat from ★ across: 32 dc and 10 ch-3 sps.

**Row 11:** Repeat Row 5: 63 sts.

**Row 12:** Ch 3, turn; dc in first sc, ch 3, ★ skip next 2 sts, dc in next 3 sts, ch 3; repeat from ★ across to last 2 sc, dc in last 2 sc: 40 dc and 13 ch-3 sps.

**Row 13:** Repeat Row 5: 81 sts.

**Row 14:** Ch 3, turn; dc in first sc, ★ ch 3, skip next 2 sts, dc in next 3 sts; repeat from ★ across: 50 dc and 16 ch-3 sps.

**Edging Rnd:** Ch 1, turn; sc in first 2 dc, 5 dc in next ch-3 sp, ★ skip next dc, sc in next dc, 5 dc in next ch-3 sp; repeat from ★ across to last 2 dc, sc in last 2 dc; working in end of rows, 5 dc in first dc row, skip next sc row, sc in next dc row, (skip next sc row, 5 dc in next dc row, skip next sc row, sc in next dc row) twice, 5 dc in next dc row, sc in next dc row, skip next dc row, 5 dc in free loop of next ch ***(Fig. 1, page 45)***, skip next dc row, sc in next dc row, 5 dc in next dc row, sc in next dc row, skip next sc row, 5 dc in next dc row, (skip next sc row, sc in next dc row, skip next sc row, 5 dc in next dc row) twice; join with slip st to first sc, finish off.

**Optional:** Paint large dots on wrong side of rug for a non-slip surface.

# Flip-Flops

EASY

**Finished Size:** 45" wide x 20½" high (114.5 cm x 52 cm)

## SHOPPING LIST

### Yarn

**Rug** (Bulky Weight) JUMBO 7
[5.29 ounces, 46 yards (150 grams, 42 meters) per skein]:

- ☐ Wintergreen - 5 skeins

**Appliqué** (Medium Weight) MEDIUM 4

- ☐ White - 45 yards (41 meters)
- ☐ Pink - 45 yards (41 meters)
- ☐ Green - 45 yards (41 meters)
- ☐ Yellow - 45 yards (41 meters)

### Crochet Hooks

**Rug**

- ☐ Size Q (16 mm) **or** size needed for gauge

**Appliqué**

- ☐ Size H (5 mm)

### Additional Supplies

- ☐ Yarn needle
- ☐ Puffy fabric paint (optional)

## GAUGE INFORMATION

**Gauge Swatch:**
9" wide x 3¾" high
(22.75 cm x 9.5 cm)
Work same as Rug for 2 rows: 12 tr.

## RUG

**Row 1** (Right side)**:** With larger size hook and Wintergreen, ch 4, 6 dc in fourth ch from hook **(3 skipped chs count as first dc)**: 7 dc.

***Note:*** Loop a short piece of yarn around any stitch to mark Row 1 as **right** side.

**Row 2:** Ch 4 **(counts as first tr, now and throughout)**, turn; tr ***(see Treble Crochet, page 44)*** in sp **before** next dc ***(Fig. 2, page 45)***, skip next dc, (2 tr in sp **before** next dc, skip next dc) 4 times, tr in sp **before** last dc and in last dc: 12 tr.

Continue working in sps **between** sts unless otherwise indicated.

**Row 3:** Ch 3 (**counts as first dc, now and throughout**), turn; dc in first sp, (2 dc in next sp, dc in next sp) 5 times, dc in last tr: 18 dc.

**Row 4:** Ch 4, turn; tr in first sp, 2 tr in next sp, (tr in next 2 sps, 2 tr in next sp) 4 times, tr in last 3 sps and in last dc: 24 tr.

**Row 5:** Ch 3, turn; dc in first 2 sps, 2 dc in next sp, (dc in next 3 sps, 2 dc in next sp) 4 times, dc in last 4 sps and in last tr: 30 dc.

**Row 6:** Ch 4, turn; tr in first 3 sps, 2 tr in next sp, (tr in next 4 sps, 2 tr in next sp) 4 times, tr in last 5 sps and in last dc: 36 tr.

**Row 7:** Ch 3, turn; dc in first 4 sps, 2 dc in next sp, (dc in next 5 sps, 2 dc in next sp) 4 times, dc in last 6 sps and in last tr: 42 dc.

**Row 8:** Ch 4, turn; tr in first 5 sps, 2 tr in next sp, (tr in next 6 sps, 2 tr in next sp) 4 times, tr in last 7 sps and in last dc: 48 tr.

**Row 9:** Ch 3, turn; dc in first 6 sps, 2 dc in next sp, (dc in next 7 sps, 2 dc in next sp) 4 times, dc in last 8 sps and in last tr: 54 dc.

**Row 10:** Ch 4, turn; tr in first 7 sps, 2 tr in next sp, (tr in next 8 sps, 2 tr in next sp) 4 times, tr in last 9 sps and in last dc: 60 tr.

**Row 11:** Ch 3, turn; dc in first 8 sps, 2 dc in next sp, (dc in next 9 sps, 2 dc in next sp) 4 times, dc in last 10 sps and in last tr: 66 dc.

**Row 12:** Ch 4, turn; tr in first 9 sps, 2 tr in next sp, (tr in next 10 sps, 2 tr in next sp) 4 times, tr in last 11 sps and in last dc: 72 tr.

**Edging Rnd:** Ch 3, turn; 2 dc in first tr, skip next tr, sc in next tr, ★ skip next tr, 5 dc in next tr, skip next tr, sc in next tr; repeat from ★ across to last tr, leave last tr unworked; working in end of rows, 5 dc in first tr row, (sc in next dc row, 5 dc in next tr row) 5 times, skip next dc row, 5 dc in free loop of next ch ***(Fig. 1, page 45)***, skip next dc row, (5 dc in next tr row, sc in next dc row) across to last tr row, 2 dc in last tr row; join with slip st to first dc, finish off.

## APPLIQUÉS

### Flip-Flop (Make 2 **each** using White, Green, Pink, and Yellow)

With smaller size hook and color indicated, ch 16.

**Rnd 1** (Right side)**:** 3 Sc in second ch from hook, sc in next 5 chs, hdc in next 4 chs, dc in next 4 chs, 7 dc in last ch; working in free loops of beginning ch, dc in next 4 chs, hdc in next 4 chs, sc in next 5 chs; join with slip st to first sc: 36 sts.

***Note:*** Mark Rnd 1 as **right** side.

**Rnd 2:** Ch 3, dc in same st as joining, 2 dc in each of next 2 sc, dc in next 14 sts, 2 dc in each of next 5 dc, dc in last 14 sts; join with slip st to first dc: 44 dc.

**Rnd 3:** Ch 3, dc in same st as joining, (dc in next dc, 2 dc in next dc) twice, dc in next 15 dc, 2 dc in next dc, (dc in next dc, 2 dc in next dc) 4 times, dc in last 15 dc; join with slip st to first dc: 52 dc.

**Rnd 4:** Ch 2 **(counts as first hdc)**, 2 hdc in same st as joining, (hdc in next 2 dc, 2 hdc in next dc) twice, hdc in next 9 dc, dc in next 7 dc, 2 dc in next dc, (dc in next 2 dc, 2 dc in next dc) 4 times, dc in next 9 dc, hdc in last 7 dc; join with slip st to first hdc, finish off.

Using photo, page 19, as a guide for placement:

- With chain stitch ***(Figs. 3a & b, page 45)*** and using a double strand of yarn, add chains to each Flip-Flop in colors shown.
- Sew **wrong** side of Appliqués to **right** side of Rug.

**Optional:** Paint large dots on wrong side of rug for a non-slip surface.

# Anchors

EASY

**Finished Size:** 45" wide x 20½" high (114.5 cm x 52 cm)

## SHOPPING LIST

### Yarn

**Rug** (Jumbo Weight) JUMBO 7
[5.29 ounces, 46 yards (150 grams, 42 meters) per skein]:

- ☐ Off White - 5 skeins

**Appliqué** (Medium Weight) MEDIUM 4

- ☐ Blue - 80 yards (73 meters)
- ☐ Grey - 10 yards (9 meters)

### Crochet Hooks

**Rug**

- ☐ Size Q (16 mm) **or** size needed for gauge

**Appliqué**

- ☐ Size I (5.5 mm)

### Additional Supplies

- ☐ Yarn needle
- ☐ Puffy fabric paint (optional)

## GAUGE INFORMATION

**Gauge Swatch:**
9" wide x 3¾" high (22.75 cm x 9.5 cm)
Work same as Rug for 2 rows: 12 tr.

## STITCH GUIDE

**SINGLE CROCHET 2 TOGETHER** ***(abbreviated sc2tog)***
Pull up a loop in each of next 2 sc, YO and draw through all 3 loops on hook **(counts as one sc)**.

**SINGLE CROCHET 3 TOGETHER** ***(abbreviated sc3tog)***
Pull up a loop in each of first 3 sc, YO and draw through all 4 loops on hook.

## RUG

With Off White, work same as Flip-Flops Rug, page 18.

## APPLIQUÉ (Make 2)

With smaller size hook and Blue, ch 9; join with slip st to form a ring.

**Foundation Rnd** (Right side)**:** Ch 3, 17 dc in ring; join with slip st to first dc: 18 dc.

*Note:* Mark Foundation Rnd as **right** side.

Begin working in rows.

**Row 1:** Ch 3, turn; dc in next 4 dc; finish off leaving remaining 13 dc unworked: 5 dc.

**Row 2:** With smaller size hook and Blue, ch 8; with **right** side facing, sc in each dc across Row 1: 5 sc and 8 chs.

**Row 3:** Ch 10, turn; dc in fourth ch from hook **(3 skipped chs count as first dc)** and in next 6 chs, dc in next 5 sc and in last 8 chs: 21 dc.

**Row 4:** Ch 3, turn; dc in next dc and in each dc across.

**Row 5:** Turn; slip st in first 9 dc, ch 3, dc in next 4 dc, leave remaining 8 dc unworked: 5 dc.

**Rows 6-16:** Ch 3, turn; dc in each dc across.

Finish off.

**Row 17:** With smaller size hook and Blue, ch 15; with **wrong** side facing, sc in each dc across Row 16: 5 sc and 15 chs.

**Row 18:** Ch 17, turn; dc in fourth ch from hook and in next 13 chs, dc in next 5 sc and in last 15 chs: 35 dc.

**Row 19:** Ch 3, turn; dc in next 4 dc, 2 dc in next dc, dc in next 5 dc, 2 dc in next dc, dc in next 11 dc, (2 dc in next dc, dc in next 5 dc) twice: 39 dc.

**Row 20:** Ch 3, turn; (dc in next 6 dc, 2 dc in next dc) twice, dc in next 9 dc, 2 dc in next dc, dc in next 6 dc, 2 dc in next dc, dc in last 7 dc: 43 dc.

## First End

**Row 1** (Right side)**:** Ch 1; work 7 sc evenly spaced across end of Rows 18-20.

**Row 2:** Ch 1, turn; beginning in first sc, sc2tog, sc in next 3 sc, sc2tog: 5 sc.

**Row 3:** Ch 1, turn; beginning in first sc, sc2tog, sc in next sc, sc2tog: 3 sc.

**Row 4:** Ch 1, turn; sc3tog; finish off leaving a long end for sewing.

## Second End

**Row 1:** With **right** side facing, using smaller size hook and working across opposite end of Rows 18-20, join Blue with sc in Row 18 ***(see Joining With Sc, page 44)***; work 6 sc evenly spaced across: 7 sc.

Complete same as First End.

Using photo as a guide for placement:

- Sew **wrong** side of Appliqués to **right** side of Rug.
- With chain stitch ***(Figs. 3a & b, page 45)*** and using a double strand of Grey, add chains to each Appliqué.

**Optional:** Paint large dots on wrong side of rug for a non-slip surface.

# Pineapple

EASY

**Finished Size:** 45" wide x 20½" high (114.5 cm x 52 cm)

## SHOPPING LIST

### Yarn

**Rug** (Jumbo Weight) JUMBO 7
[5.29 ounces, 46 yards (150 grams, 42 meters) per skein]:

- ☐ Tan - 5 skeins

**Appliqué** (Medium Weight) MEDIUM 4

- ☐ Gold - 60 yards (55 meters)
- ☐ Green - 25 yards (23 meters)

### Crochet Hooks

**Rug**

- ☐ Size Q (16 mm) **or** size needed for gauge

**Appliqué**

- ☐ Size H (5 mm)

### Additional Supplies

- ☐ Yarn needle
- ☐ Puffy fabric paint (optional)

## GAUGE INFORMATION

**Gauge Swatch:**
9" wide x 3¾" high
(22.75 cm x 9.5 cm)
Work same as Rug for 2 rows: 12 tr.

## STITCH GUIDE

**DOUBLE CROCHET 2 TOGETHER** ***(abbreviated dc2tog)***
(uses next 2 sts)
★ YO, insert hook in **next** st, YO and pull up a loop, YO and draw through 2 loops on hook; repeat from ★ once **more**, YO and draw through all 3 loops on hook (**counts as one dc**).

## RUG

With Tan, work same as Flip-Flops Rug, page 18.

## APPLIQUÉ

### Pineapple

With smaller size hook and Gold, ch 22.

**Row 1** (Right side)**:** Dc in fourth ch from hook **(3 skipped chs count as first dc)** and in each ch across: 20 dc.

*Note:* Mark Row 1 as **right** side.

**Row 2:** Ch 1, turn; sc in first dc, tr in next dc, (sc in next dc pushing tr to **right** side, tr in next dc) across to last 2 dc, sc in last 2 dc pushing tr to **right** side.

**Row 3** (Increase row)**:** Ch 3 **(counts as first dc, now and throughout)**, turn; dc in first sc and in each st across to last sc, 2 dc in last sc: 22 dc.

**Rows 4-8:** Repeat Rows 2 and 3 twice, then repeat Row 2 once **more**: 26 sts.

**Row 9:** Ch 3, turn; dc in next sc and in each st across.

**Row 10:** Ch 1, turn; sc in first dc, tr in next dc, (sc in next dc pushing tr to **right** side, tr in next dc) across to last 2 dc, sc in last 2 dc pushing tr to **right** side.

**Rows 11-18:** Repeat Rows 9 and 10, 4 times.

**Row 19** (Decrease row)**:** Ch 3, turn; dc2tog, dc in next st and in each st across to last 3 sts, dc2tog, dc in last sc: 24 dc.

**Row 20:** Ch 1, turn; sc in first dc, tr in next dc, (sc in next dc pushing tr to **right** side, tr in next dc) across to last 2 dc, sc in last 2 dc pushing tr to **right** side.

**Rows 21 and 22:** Repeat Rows 19 and 20; at end of Row 22, finish off: 22 dc.

**Leaf** (Make 8)
With smaller size hook and Green, ch 20; tr in fifth ch from hook and in next 2 chs, dc in next 4 chs, hdc in next 4 chs, sc in next 4 chs, 3 sc in last ch; working in free loops of beginning ch *(Fig. 1, page 45)*, sc in next 4 chs, hdc in next 4 chs, dc in next 4 chs, tr in next 4 chs; finish off leaving a long end for sewing.

Using photo as a guide for placement:

- Sew **wrong** side of Pineapple to **right** side of Rug.
- Arrange Leaves at top of Pineapple, overlapping as desired to achieve different heights; sew Leaves in place.

**Optional:** Paint large dots on wrong side of rug for a non-slip surface.

# Antlers

EASY

**Finished Size:** 44" wide x 21" deep (112 cm x 53.5 cm)

## SHOPPING LIST

### Yarn (Super Bulky Weight) SUPER BULKY 6

**Rug**

[8 ounces, 160 yards (227 grams, 146 meters) per skein]:

- ☐ Brown - 4 skeins
- ☐ Green - 4 skeins

**Appliqué**

[5.3 ounces, 108 yards (150 grams, 98 meters) per skein]:

- ☐ Tan - 1 skein

### Crochet Hooks

**Rug**

- ☐ Size Q (16 mm) **or** size needed for gauge

**Appliqué**

- ☐ Size K (6.5 mm)

### Additional Supplies

- ☐ Yarn needle
- ☐ Puffy fabric paint (optional)

## GAUGE INFORMATION

**Gauge Swatch:**

8½" wide x 3¾" high
(21.5 cm x 9.5 cm)

Work same as Rug for 2 rows: 12 tr.

## RUG

**Row 1** (Right side)**:** With larger size hook and holding one strand of Green and one strand of Brown together, ch 4, 6 dc in fourth ch from hook **(3 skipped chs count as first dc)**: 7 dc.

***Note:*** Loop a short piece of yarn around any stitch to mark Row 1 as **right** side.

NOBODY'S FOOL
NORTHWEST CORNER

**Row 2:** Ch 4 **(counts as first tr, now and throughout)**, turn; tr ***(see Treble Crochet, page 44)*** in sp **before** next dc ***(Fig. 2, page 45)***, skip next dc, (2 tr in sp **before** next dc, skip next dc) 4 times, tr in sp **before** last dc and in last dc: 12 tr.

Continue working in sps **between** sts unless otherwise indicated.

**Row 3:** Ch 3 **(counts as first dc, now and throughout)**, turn; dc in first sp, (2 dc in next sp, dc in next sp) 5 times, dc in last tr: 18 dc.

**Row 4:** Ch 4, turn; tr in first sp, 2 tr in next sp, (tr in next 2 sps, 2 tr in next sp) 4 times, tr in last 3 sps and in last dc: 24 tr.

**Row 5:** Ch 3, turn; dc in first 2 sps, 2 dc in next sp, (dc in next 3 sps, 2 dc in next sp) 4 times, dc in last 4 sps and in last tr: 30 dc.

**Row 6:** Ch 4, turn; tr in first 3 sps, 2 tr in next sp, (tr in next 4 sps, 2 tr in next sp) 4 times, tr in last 5 sps and in last dc: 36 tr.

**Row 7:** Ch 3, turn; dc in first 4 sps, 2 dc in next sp, (dc in next 5 sps, 2 dc in next sp) 4 times, dc in last 6 sps and in last tr: 42 dc.

**Row 8:** Ch 4, turn; tr in first 5 sps, 2 tr in next sp, (tr in next 6 sps, 2 tr in next sp) 4 times, tr in last 7 sps and in last dc: 48 tr.

**Row 9:** Ch 3, turn; dc in first 6 sps, 2 dc in next sp, (dc in next 7 sps, 2 dc in next sp) 4 times, dc in last 8 sps and in last tr: 54 dc.

**Row 10:** Ch 4, turn; tr in first 7 sps, 2 tr in next sp, (tr in next 8 sps, 2 tr in next sp) 4 times, tr in last 9 sps and in last dc: 60 tr.

**Row 11:** Ch 3, turn; dc in first 8 sps, 2 dc in next sp, (dc in next 9 sps, 2 dc in next sp) 4 times, dc in last 10 sps and in last tr: 66 dc.

**Row 12:** Ch 4, turn; tr in first 9 sps, 2 tr in next sp, (tr in next 10 sps, 2 tr in next sp) 4 times, tr in last 11 sps and in last dc: 72 tr.

**Edging Rnd:** Ch 3, turn; 2 dc in first tr, skip next tr, sc in next tr, ★ skip next tr, 5 dc in next tr, skip next tr, sc in next tr; repeat from ★ across to last tr, leave last tr unworked; working in end of rows, 5 dc in first tr row, (sc in next dc row, 5 dc in next tr row) 5 times, skip next dc row, 5 dc in free loop of next ch ***(Fig. 1, page 45)***, skip next dc row, (5 dc in next tr row, sc in next dc row) across to last tr row, 2 dc in last tr row; join with slip st to first dc, finish off.

## APPLIQUÉ (Make 2)

With smaller size hook and Tan, ch 50.

**Row 1** (Main Antler)**:** Dc in fourth ch from hook **(3 skipped chs count as first dc)** and in each ch across: 48 dc.

**Row 2:** Ch 1, turn; sc in first 10 dc, ch 31, sc in second ch from hook and in next 14 chs, hdc in last 15 chs; sc in next 10 dc on Main Antler, ch 15, sc in second ch from hook and in next 4 chs, hdc in last 9 chs; sc in next 10 dc on Main Antler, ch 21, sc in second ch from hook and in next 9 chs, hdc in last 10 chs; sc in next 10 dc on Main Antler, ch 10, sc in second ch from hook and in next 4 chs, hdc in last 4 chs; sc in last 8 dc on Main Antler; finish off leaving a long end for sewing.

Using photo as a guide for placement, sew Appliqués to **right** side of Rug.

**Optional:** Paint large dots on wrong side of rug for a non-slip surface.

# Sunflowers

EASY

**Finished Size:** 44" wide x 21" deep (112 cm x 53.5 cm)

## SHOPPING LIST

### Yarn

**Rug** (Super Bulky Weight) SUPER BULKY 6
[5 ounces, 81 yards
(142 grams, 74 meters) per
skein]:

- ☐ Green - 7 skeins

**Appliqué** (Medium Weight) MEDIUM 4
[6 ounces, 315 yards
(170.1 grams, 288 meters) per
skein]:

- ☐ Yellow - 1 skein
- ☐ Brown - 50 yards (46 meters)

### Crochet Hooks

**Rug**

- ☐ Size Q (16 mm)
  **or** size needed for gauge

**Appliqué**

- ☐ Size H (5 mm)

### Additional Supplies

- ☐ Yarn needle
- ☐ Puffy fabric paint (optional)

## GAUGE INFORMATION

**Gauge Swatch:**
8½" wide x 3¾" high
(21.5 cm x 9.5 cm)
Work same as Rug for 2 rows: 12 tr.

## RUG

Holding two strands of Green together, work same as Antlers Rug, page 30.

## APPLIQUÉ (Make 3)

### Center

**Rnd 1** (Wrong side)**:** With smaller size hook and Brown, ch 4, 11 dc in fourth ch from hook **(3 skipped chs count as first dc)**; join with slip st to first dc: 12 dc.

***Note:*** Mark the **back** of any stitch on Rnd 1 to mark **right** side.

**Rnd 2:** Ch 1, (sc, tr) in same st as joining and in each dc around pushing tr to **right** side; join with slip st to first sc: 24 sts.

**Rnd 3:** Ch 1, (sc, tr) in same st as joining, sc in next st pushing tr to **right** side, ★ (sc, tr) in next st, sc in next st pushing tr to **right** side; repeat from ★ around; join with slip st to first sc: 36 sts.

**Rnd 4:** Ch 1, sc in same st as joining and in next st, (sc, tr) in next st, ★ sc in next 2 sts pushing tr to **right** side, (sc, tr) in next st; repeat from ★ around; join with slip st to first sc: 48 sts.

**Rnd 5:** Ch 1, sc in same st as joining, tr in next st, (sc in next st pushing tr to **right** side, tr in next st) around; join with slip st to first sc pushing tr to **right** side, finish off.

## Petals

**Rnd 1:** With **right** side facing and using smaller size hook, join Yellow with dc in any st ***(see Joining With Dc, page 44)***; dc in same st and in next 3 sts, (2 dc in next st, dc in next 3 sts) around; join with slip st to first dc: 60 dc.

**Rnd 2:** Ch 1, ★ sc in sp **before** next dc, skip next 4 dc, 6 dc around post of next dc (from bottom to top), 6 dc around post of next dc (from top to bottom), skip next 4 dc; repeat from ★ around; join with slip st to first sc: 6 Petals.

**Rnd 3:** Ch 3, dc in same st as joining, working **behind** Petals and in dc on Rnd 1, dc in next 4 dc, (2 dc in next dc, dc in next 4 dc) around; join with slip st to first dc: 72 dc.

**Rnd 4:** Ch 1, ★ sc in sp **before** next dc, skip next 3 dc, 6 dc around post of next dc (from bottom to top), 6 dc around post of next dc (from top to bottom), skip next 3 dc; repeat from ★ around; join with slip st to first sc: 9 Petals.

**Rnd 5:** Ch 3, working **behind** Petals and in dc on Rnd 3, dc in next 7 dc, 2 dc in next dc, (dc in next 8 dc, 2 dc in next dc) around; join with slip st to first dc: 80 dc.

**Rnd 6:** Repeat Rnd 4: 10 Petals.

**Rnd 7:** Ch 3, working **behind** Petals and in dc on Rnd 5, dc in next 6 dc, 2 dc in next dc, (dc in next 7 dc, 2 dc in next dc) around; join with slip st to first dc: 90 dc.

**Rnd 8:** Repeat Rnd 2; finish off leaving a long end for sewing: 9 Petals.

Using photo as a guide for placement, sew **wrong** side of Appliqués to **right** side of Rug.

**Optional:** Paint large dots on wrong side of rug for a non-slip surface.

# Wine Glasses

EASY

**Finished Size:** 44" wide x 21" deep (112 cm x 53.5 cm)

## SHOPPING LIST

### Yarn

**Rug** (Super Bulky Weight)
[5 ounces, 81 yards
(142 grams, 74 meters) per skein]:

- ☐ Grey - 7 skeins

**Appliqué** (Medium Weight)

- ☐ Red - 70 yards (64 meters)
- ☐ White - 40 yards (36.5 meters)

### Crochet Hooks

**Rug**

- ☐ Size Q (16 mm)
  **or** size needed for gauge

**Appliqué**

- ☐ Size H (5 mm)

### Additional Supplies

- ☐ Yarn needle
- ☐ Puffy fabric paint (optional)

## GAUGE INFORMATION

**Gauge Swatch:**
8½" wide x 3¾" high
(21.5 cm x 9.5 cm)
Work same as Rug for 2 rows: 12 tr.

## RUG

Holding two strands of Grey together, work same as Antlers Rug, page 30.

## APPLIQUÉ (Make 2)

### Stem

Using smaller size hook and a single strand of White, ch 25.

**Row 1** (Wrong side)**:** Dc in fourth ch from hook **(3 skipped chs count as first dc)** and in each ch across: 23 dc.

***Note:*** Mark the **back** of any stitch on Row 1 to mark **right** side.

**Row 2:** Turn; slip st in first 4 dc, sc in next 3 dc, hdc in next 2 dc, dc in next 5 dc, hdc in next 2 dc, sc in next 3 dc, slip st in next dc, leave remaining 3 dc unworked: 20 sts.

**Row 3:** Turn; skip first slip st, slip st in next 3 sc, sc in next hdc, hdc in next hdc, dc in next 5 dc, hdc in next hdc, sc in next hdc, slip st in next sc, leave remaining 6 sts unworked: 13 sts.

**Row 4:** Turn; skip first slip st, slip st in next 3 sts, ch 3 **(counts as first dc)**, dc in next 4 dc, leave remaining 5 sts unworked: 5 dc.

**Rows 5-10:** Ch 3, turn; dc in next 4 dc.

**Row 11:** Ch 3, turn; 2 dc in first dc, dc in next 3 dc, 3 dc in last dc; finish off: 9 dc.

## Glass

**Row 1:** With **right** side facing and using smaller size hook, join Red with dc in first dc *(see Joining With Dc, page 44)*; dc in next dc and in each dc across.

**Rows 2 and 3:** Ch 3, turn; 2 dc in first dc, dc in next dc and in each dc across to last dc, 3 dc in last dc: 17 dc.

**Row 4:** Ch 3, turn; dc in next dc and in each dc across.

**Row 5** (Increase row)**:** Ch 3, turn; dc in first dc and in each dc across to last dc, 2 dc in last dc: 19 dc.

**Rows 6-9:** Repeat Rows 4 and 5 twice: 23 dc.

**Row 10-12:** Ch 3, turn; dc in next dc and in each dc across.

Finish off leaving a long end for sewing.

Using photo as a guide for placement, sew **wrong** side of Appliqués to **right** side of Rug.

**Optional:** Paint large dots on wrong side of rug for a non-slip surface.

# General Instructions

## ABBREVIATIONS

| | |
|---|---|
| ch(s) | chain(s) |
| cm | centimeters |
| dc | double crochet(s) |
| dc2tog | double crochet 2 together |
| dc4tog | double crochet 4 together |
| dc7tog | double crochet 7 together |
| hdc | half double crochet(s) |
| mm | millimeters |
| Rnd(s) | Round(s) |
| sc | single crochet(s) |
| sc2tog | single crochet 2 together |
| sc3tog | single crochet 3 together |
| sp(s) | space(s) |
| st(s) | stitch(es) |
| tr | treble crochet(s) |
| YO | yarn over |

## SYMBOLS & TERMS

★ — work instructions following ★ as many **more** times as indicated in addition to the first time.

( ) or **[ ]** — work enclosed instructions **as many** times as specified by the number immediately following **or** work all enclosed instructions in the stitch or space indicated **or** contains explanatory remarks.

colon (:) — the number(s) given after a colon at the end of a row or round denote(s) the number of stitches or spaces you should have on that row or round.

| CROCHET TERMINOLOGY | | |
|---|---|---|
| UNITED STATES | | INTERNATIONAL |
| slip stitch (slip st) | = | single crochet (sc) |
| single crochet (sc) | = | double crochet (dc) |
| half double crochet (hdc) | = | half treble crochet (htr) |
| double crochet (dc) | = | treble crochet (tr) |
| treble crochet (tr) | = | double treble crochet (dtr) |
| double treble crochet (dtr) | = | triple treble crochet (ttr) |
| triple treble crochet (tr tr) | = | quadruple treble crochet (qtr) |
| skip | = | miss |

| | |
|---|---|
| BEGINNER | Projects for first-time crocheters using basic stitches. Minimal shaping. |
| EASY | Projects using yarn with basic stitches, repetitive stitch patterns, simple color changes, and simple shaping and finishing. |
| INTERMEDIATE | Projects using a variety of techniques, such as basic lace patterns or color patterns, mid-level shaping and finishing. |
| EXPERIENCED | Projects with intricate stitch patterns, techniques and dimension, such as non-repeating patterns, multi-color techniques, fine threads, small hooks, detailed shaping and refined finishing. |

| Yarn Weight Symbol & Names | LACE 0 | SUPER FINE 1 | FINE 2 | LIGHT 3 | MEDIUM 4 | BULKY 5 | SUPER BULKY 6 | JUMBO 7 |
|---|---|---|---|---|---|---|---|---|
| Type of Yarns in Category | Fingering, size 10 crochet thread | Sock, Fingering, Baby | Sport, Baby | DK, Light Worsted | Worsted, Afghan, Aran | Chunky, Craft, Rug | Super Bulky, Roving | Jumbo, Roving |
| Crochet Gauge* Ranges in Single Crochet to 4" (10 cm) | 32-42 sts** | 21-32 sts | 16-20 sts | 12-17 sts | 11-14 sts | 8-11 sts | 6-9 sts | 5 sts and fewer |
| Advised Hook Size Range | Steel*** 6 to 8, Regular hook B-1 | B-1 to E-4 | E-4 to 7 | 7 to I-9 | I-9 to K-10½ | K-10½ to M/N-13 | M/N-13 to Q | Q and larger |

*GUIDELINES ONLY: The chart above reflects the most commonly used gauges and hook sizes for specific yarn categories.

** Lace weight yarns are usually crocheted with larger hooks to create lacy openwork patterns. Accordingly, a gauge range is difficult to determine. Always follow the gauge stated in your pattern.

*** Steel crochet hooks are sized differently from regular hooks–the higher the number, the smaller the hook, which is the reverse of regular hook sizing.

## GAUGE

Exact gauge is **essential** for proper size. Before beginning your Rug, make the sample swatch given in the individual instructions in the yarn and hook specified. If your swatch is larger or smaller than specified, **make another, changing hook size to get the correct gauge**. Keep trying until you find the size hook that will give you the specified gauge.

## JOINING WITH SC

When instructed to join with sc, begin with a slip knot on hook. Insert hook in stitch or space indicated, YO and pull up a loop, YO and draw through both loops on hook.

## JOINING WITH DC

When instructed to join with dc, begin with a slip knot on hook. YO, holding loop on hook, insert hook in stitch or space indicated, YO and pull up a loop (3 loops on hook), (YO and draw through 2 loops on hook) twice.

## TREBLE CROCHET

### *(abbreviated tr)*

YO, insert hook in st or sp indicated, YO and pull up a loop (4 loops on hook), (YO and draw through 2 loops on hook) 3 times.

| CROCHET HOOKS | |
|---|---|
| **U.S.** | **Metric mm** |
| B-1 | 2.25 |
| C-2 | 2.75 |
| D-3 | 3.25 |
| E-4 | 3.5 |
| F-5 | 3.75 |
| G-6 | 4 |
| 7 | 4.5 |
| H-8 | 5 |
| I-9 | 5.5 |
| J-10 | 6 |
| K-10½ | 6.5 |
| L-11 | 8 |
| M/N-13 | 9 |
| N/P-15 | 10 |
| P/Q | 15 |
| Q | 16 |
| S | 19 |

## FREE LOOPS OF A CHAIN

When instructed to work in free loops of a chain, work in loop indicated by arrow *(Fig. 1)*.

**Fig. 1**

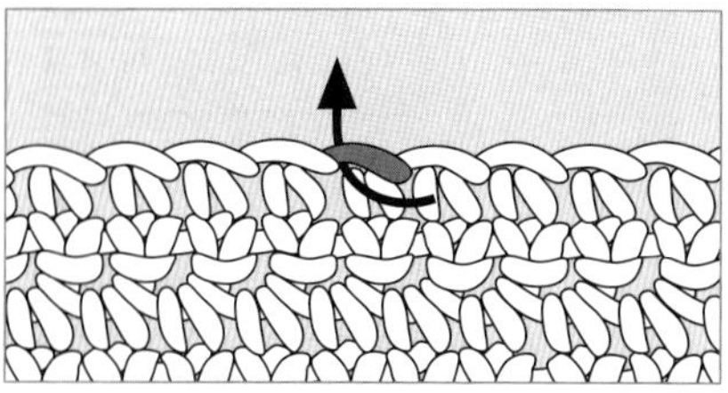

## WORKING IN SPACE BEFORE A STITCH

When instructed to work in space **before** a stitch or in spaces **between** stitches, insert hook in space indicated by arrow *(Fig. 2)*.

**Fig. 2**

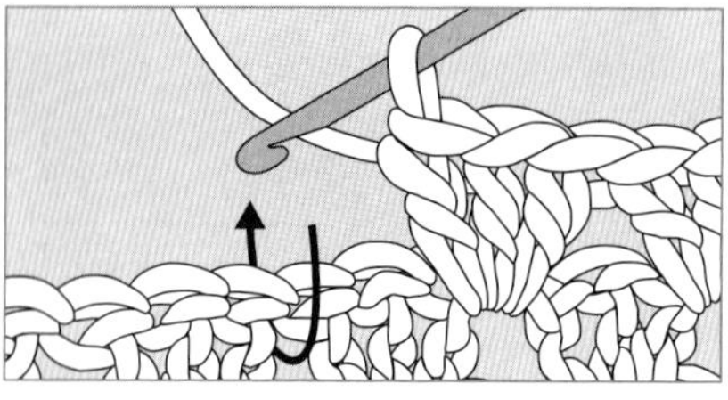

## CHAIN STITCH

Chain stitch is worked from **right** to **left**. Make all stitches equal in length. Come up at 1 and make a counterclockwise loop with the yarn. Go down at 1 and come up at 2, keeping the yarn below the point of the needle *(Fig. 3a)*. Make a loop with the yarn and go down at 2; come up at 3, keeping yarn below the point of the needle *(Fig. 3b)*. Secure last loop by bringing yarn over loop and down to **wrong** side.

**Fig. 3a**

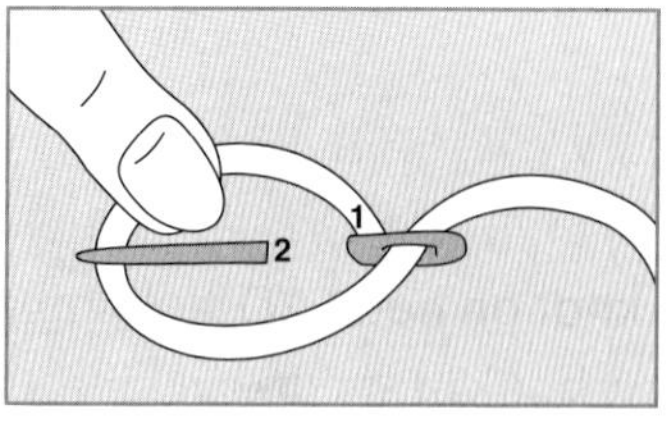


**Fig. 3b**

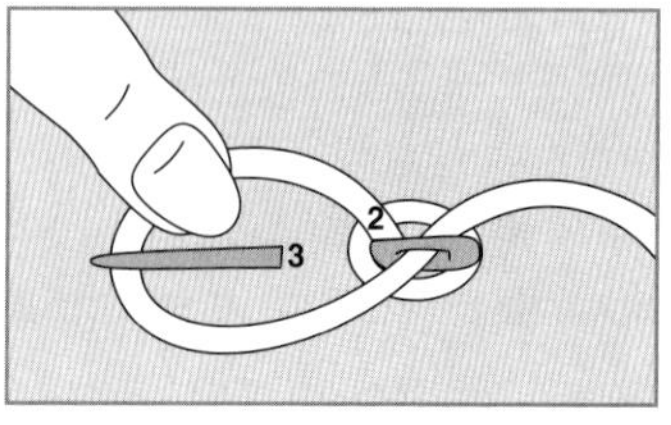

# Yarn Information

The Rugs in this book were made using a variety of yarn weights. Any brand of the specific weight of yarn may be used. It is best to refer to the yardage/meters when determining how many balls or skeins to purchase. Remember, it is not the brand of yarn that matters, but the GAUGE/TENSION that is important.

For your convenience, listed on the following page are the yarns used to create out photography models. Because yarn manufacturers make frequent changes in their product lines, you may sometimes find it necessary to use a substitute yarn or to search for the discontinued product at alternate suppliers (locally or online).

**PUFF STITCH**

*Lion Brand® Hometown USA®*

#222 Salem Creek

**LAZY PUFF STITCH**

*Lion Brand® Hometown USA®*

#305 Cape Cod Tweed

**CIRCLE**

*Red Heart® Grande™*

Tan - #307 Oatmeal

Pink - #901 Currant

**SEMI-CIRCLE**

*Red Heart® Grande™*

#275 Nectar

**FLIP-FLOPS**

*Red Heart® Grande™*

Wintergreen - #511 Wintergreen

*Caron® Simply Soft®*

White - #9701 White

Pink - #9775 Neon Pink

Green - #9770 Cool Green

Yellow - #9776 Lemonade

**ANCHORS**

*Red Heart® Grande™*

Off White - #110 Aran

*Red Heart® Soft®*

Blue - #9851 Royal Blue

*Caron® Simply Soft®*

Grey - #9509 Grey Heather

**PINEAPPLE**

*Red Heart® Grande™*

Tan - #307 Oatmeal

*Caron® Simply Soft®*

Gold - #9782 Gold

Green - #9707 Dark Sage

**ANTLERS**

*Lion Brand® Homespun®*
*Thick & Quick®*

Brown - #381 Barley

Green - #410 Herb Garden

*Bernat® Blanket™*

Tan - #00014 Sand

**SUNFLOWERS**

*Lion Brand® Hometown USA®*

Green - #172 Oklahoma City Green

*Caron® Simply Soft®*

Yellow - #9755 Sunshine

Brown - #9750 Chocolate

**WINE GLASSES**

*Lion Brand® Hometown USA®*

Grey - #149 Dallas Grey

*Caron® Simply Soft®*

Red - #9762 Burgundy

White - #9701 White

# Meet Karen Barnes

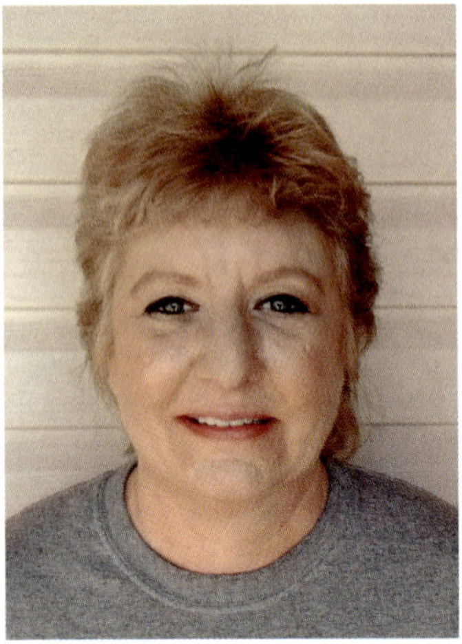

Karen Barnes is an avid yarn-lover who has been crocheting since the age of 12, taught by her grandmother and later inspired by pattern stitch encyclopedias.

The school bus driver and mother of two grown children says she likes designing home accessories such as afghans, rugs, placemats, and pillows.

Karen also enjoys sewing and traveling with her husband and mother.



Production Team: Instructional/Technical Editor - Linda A. Daley; Editorial Writer - Susan Frantz Wiles; Senior Graphic Artist - Lora Puls; Photo Stylist - Lori Wenger; and Photographer - Jason Masters.



Made in U.S.A.